Paper Quilling Patterns Step by Step

Quilling Technique Guide Book Beginners Can Follow Easily

Copyright © 2021

All rights reserved.

DEDICATION

The author and publisher have provided this e-book to you for your personal use only. You may not make this e-book publicly available in any way. Copyright infringement is against the law. If you believe the copy of this e-book you are reading infringes on the author's copyright, please notify the publisher at: https://us.macmillan.com/piracy

Paper Quilling Patterns Step by Step

Contents

What Is Quilling? 1
Basics of Quilling Paper 11
    Materials: 11
    Directions: 12
Rolled Paper Shapes to Start with 16
    Teardrop 22
    Teardrop Variations 24
    Marquis 29
    Tulip 32
    Slug 33
    Square or Diamond 35
    Square Variations 36
    Rectangle 38
    Rectangle Variations 40
    Semi-Circle 42
    Triangle 44
    Triangle Variation 46
    Arrow 47
    Arrowhead 50
    Heart 52
    Pentagon and Star 54
    Holly Leaf 58

What Is Quilling?

Quilling or paper filigree is an art form that involves the use of strips of paper that are rolled, shaped, and glued together to create decorative designs. The paper is rolled, looped, curled, twisted and otherwise manipulated to create shapes which make up designs to decorate greetings cards, pictures, boxes, eggs, and to make models, jewelry, mobiles etc. Quilling starts with rolling a strip of paper into a coil and then pinching the coil into shapes that can be glued together. There are advanced techniques and different sized paper that are used to create 3D miniatures, abstract art, flowers and portraits among many things.

History

Although its exact origins are a mystery the art of quilling is thought to have originated in Ancient Egypt. More recently quilling has been practiced as an art form in Renaissance France/Italy as well as in 18th century England During the Renaissance, French and Italian nuns and monks used quilling to decorate book covers and religious items. The paper most commonly used was strips of paper trimmed from the gilded edges of books. These gilded paper strips were then rolled to create the quilled shapes. Quilling often imitated the original ironwork of the day. In the 18th century, quilling became popular in Europe where gentle ladies of quality ("ladies of leisure") practiced the art. It was one of the few things ladies could do that was thought not too taxing for their minds or gentle dispositions. Quilling also spread to the Americas and there are a few examples from Colonial times.

Many quilled art can be found on cabinets and stands, cribbage boards, ladies' purses, a wide range of both pictures and frames, work baskets, tea caddies, coats of arms and wine coasters. Storage boxes, larger than most jewelry boxes with drawers and/or tops that opened, quilled lock boxes, and more popular is quilling jewelry in recent times became a trend for fashion lovers, as they can be very light and easy to carry on them. Some items were specially designed for quilling with recessed surfaces. Quilling was also combined or married with other techniques such as embroidery and painting.

Today, quilling is seeing a resurgence in popularity. It is sometimes used for decorating wedding invitations, for Christmas, birth announcements, greeting cards, scrapbook pages, and boxes. Quilling can be found in art galleries in Europe and in the United States and is an art that is practiced around the world.

Tools

Slotted tool

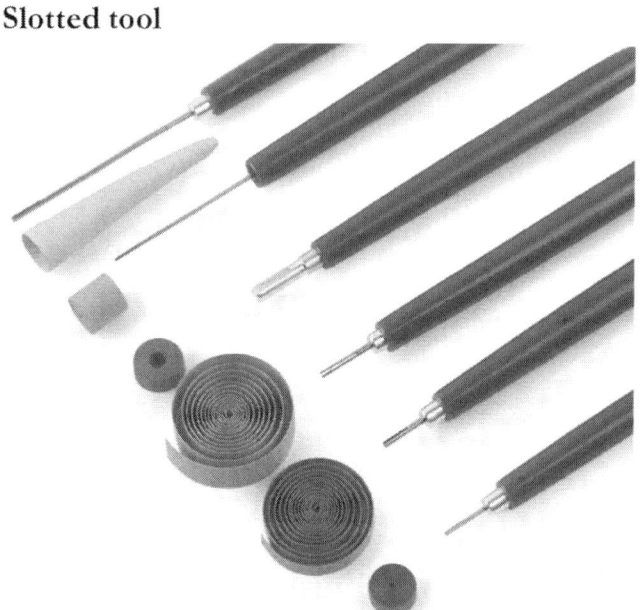

The slotted tool is the most important quilling tool as it makes curling coils much easier and faster. The quality of the coil is noticeably higher compared to a coil that was curled with a toothpick or hand. For younger children, it is recommended that a Curling Coach be used with the slotted tool.

Needle tool

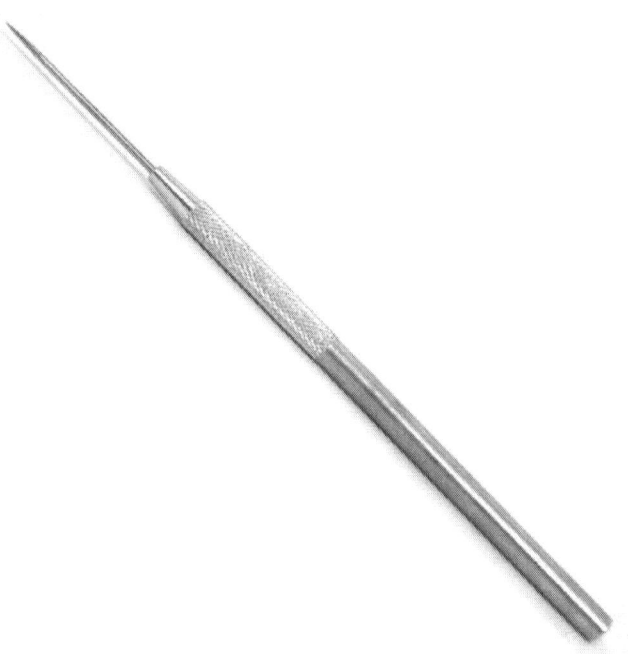

The needle tool plays a supporting role in the craft. It is used primarily to apply glue to hard-to-reach areas of the coil or quilling design.

Tweezers

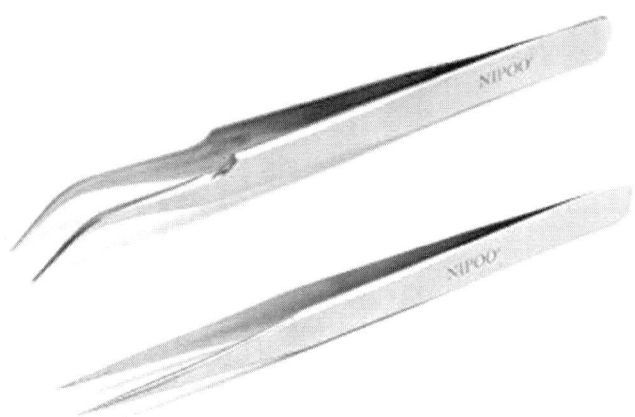

Tweezers are used to make delicate coils to prevent warping and unraveling. They keep the coils the same size which is important when making something with duplicate coils, like flower petals. Tweezers are also helpful in inserting paper in tight spaces.

Circle sizer ruler

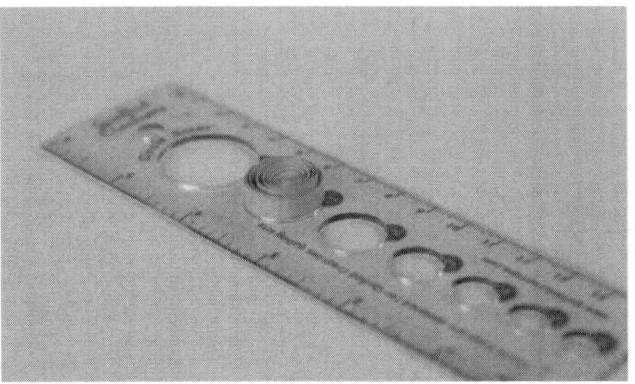

The circle sizer ruler is not essential in making coils into a desired size after curling. The ruler on the side is used to measure each strip to ensure they are the same length before curling.

Curling coach

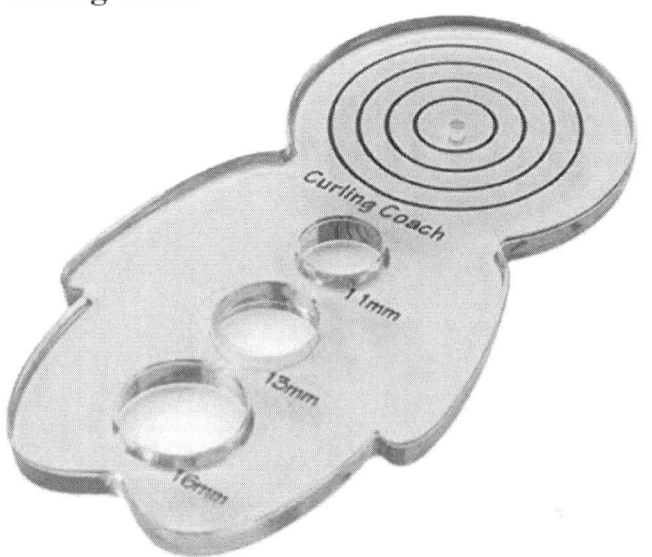

Curling coaches make a great complement tool for slotted tools and are recommended for younger kids and people who like to quill 3D miniatures. It makes curling the strips much faster and easier than if they were curled with just the slotted tool.

Crimper tool

This tool is used to make crimped quilling strips. It helps to create different patterns.

Paper Types

Quilling paper is available on the consumer market in over 250 colors and dimensions. It can be divided into various categories, like solid colored, graduated, two-tone, acid-free, and other assorted parcels of quilling paper. It is available in various dimensions, such as 1/8", ¼" and 3/8" or 3mm, 5mm, 7mm and 10mm paper parcels.[8] 5mm being the most widely used size.

Acid-Free

As the name clearly indicates this is a paper that is completely acid free. The quality makes it an outstanding choice for making scrapbooks, rubber stamping, and creating frames for pictures. It assures your project will last a lifetime, without any side effects on the framed picture or album.

Graduated

This type of paper provides an exceptional look to decorative quilling projects. The edges have a solid color that gradually fades to white. When using a graduated paper, a quilling ring begins with a dark shade but ends up being faded to a lighter side. On the contrary, some graduated papers begin as white, or a lighter shade, and then slowly fades into a solid, darker color.

Two-Tone

This is another important type of quilling paper. It is quite similar to the graduated quilling paper in its use. The look consists of a concrete color on one side and comparatively lighter color on the other side. With two-tone paper the color remains same, however the intensity of color is different. The main use of this quilling paper is to provide a desired level of softness to the quilled subject. It possesses the capacity to quill many papers in a single spiral.

Basics of Quilling Paper

Materials:

- Quilling paper: 1/8", standard width
- Quilling tool needle tool or slotted tool
- Ruler
- Scissors
- Tweezers
- Glue clear-drying, suitable for paper
- Plastic lid to use as a glue palette
- T-pin, paper piercing tool, or round toothpick
- Glass-head straight pins
- Non-stick work board, cork, or styrofoam something into which you can stick pins
- Damp cloth to keep fingers free of glue

Directions:

When purchasing a tool there are 2 basic types: a slotted tool and needle tool. The slotted tool is easiest to use; its only disadvantage is that the slot leaves a tiny crimp in the center of the coil. If this is bothersome, purchase an ultra-fine slotted tool or try a needle tool. The needle tool is a bit more difficult to master, but the reward will be a coil with a perfectly round center.

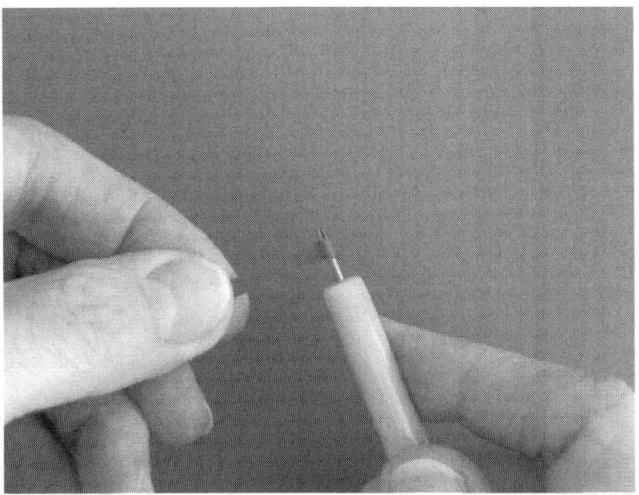

To roll a coil with a slotted tool: Slide the very end of a strip into the slot, and turn the tool with one hand while evenly guiding the strip with the other.

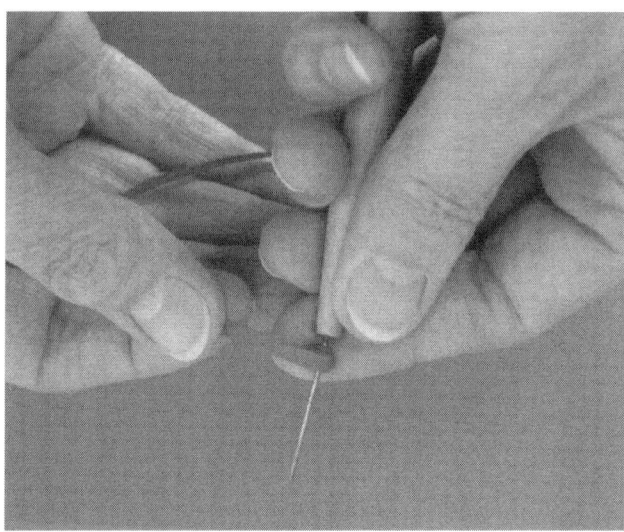

To roll a coil with a needle tool: Dampen fingers and curve one end of a strip across the needle. Roll the strip around the needle with the thumb and index finger of whichever hand feels most comfortable, applying even, firm pressure, while holding the handle of the tool with the other hand. Be sure to roll the paper, not the tool.

Whether using a slotted tool or needle tool, when

the strip is fully rolled, allow the coil to relax, slide it off the tool, and glue the end. Use only a very small amount of glue, applying it with the tip of a T-pin, paper piercing tool, or toothpick. Hold the end in place for a few moments while the glue dries. This is called a loose coil, and it's the basic shape from which many other shapes are made.

Rolled Paper Shapes to Start with

What You Need

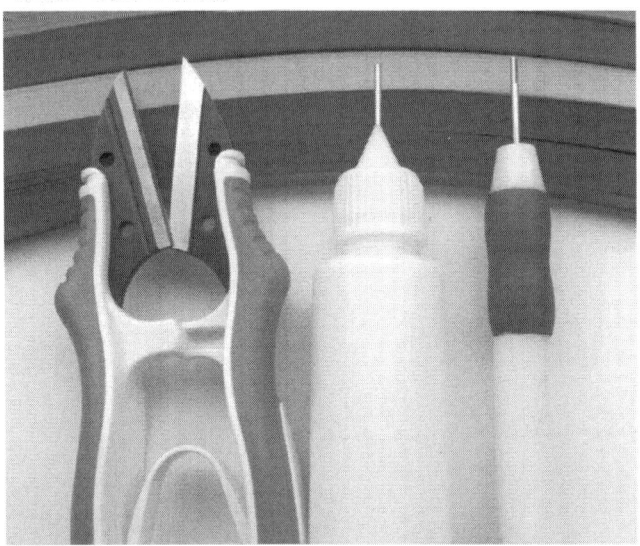

- A slotted quilling tool
- Quilling glue in a needle-tip bottle
- Scissors
- Tweezers
- Package of quilling paper strips — for beginners, I recommend ¼-inch wide (it's easy to grip and manipulate); once you've mastered the basic shapes, you may prefer

narrower strips. Cut the strips 8½-inches long for this tutorial.

Open and Closed Coils

Simple circles are the basis for most other shapes you'll create.

1. Insert Paper Into the Tool

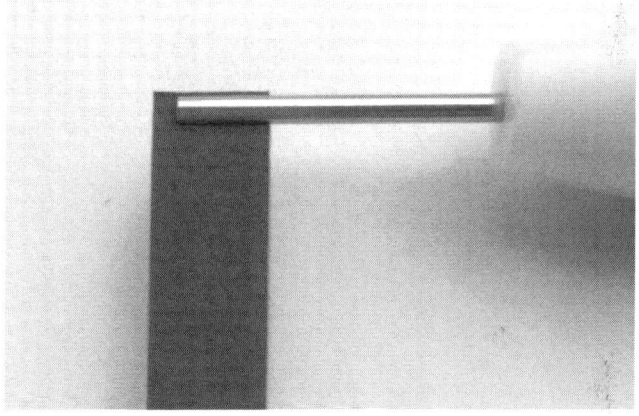

Insert a piece of quilling paper into the slot of your quilling tool; try to line up the edge of the paper with the edge of the slot as perfectly as you can. A slotted tool will naturally leave a small crimp in the center of your coil. If you'd like the crimp to be more visible, allow the paper to hang slightly over the edge.

2. Start Rollin'

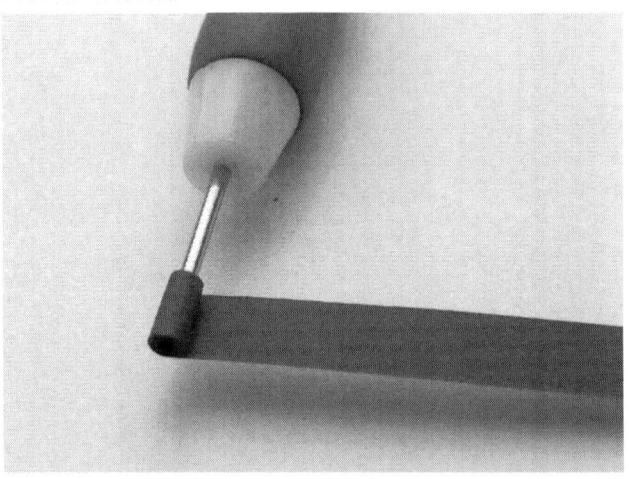

Roll the tool with your dominant hand either towards your body or away from it (whichever feels most comfortable), while holding the strip taut with your other hand.

3. Glue It

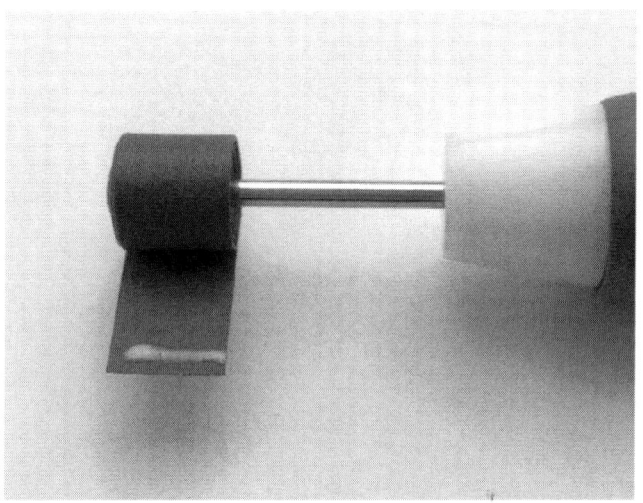

For a closed coil: When you're almost done coiling, place a dab of glue near the end of the strip and roll to complete. You don't want it to expand after you remove it from the tool.

For an open coil: Finish the coil, then remove it from the tool and allow it to expand. Once it has fully expanded, add a dab of glue and press the strip down carefully to secure.

Paper Quilling Patterns Step by Step

Teardrop

Make an open coil, then place it between the thumb and forefinger of your non-dominant hand. Arrange the inside coils evenly or however you'd like.

With your dominant hand, pinch the paper where you want the point to be to create a teardrop shape.

Teardrop Variations

Basic shapes can be manipulated to create even more shapes. The teardrop is an excellent example of this.

By slightly curving the teardrop around your thumb as you shape it, you can create a subtle shift in form without compromising the center coils. To exaggerate this effect, you can wrap the teardrop around your quilling tool or another cylindrical object.

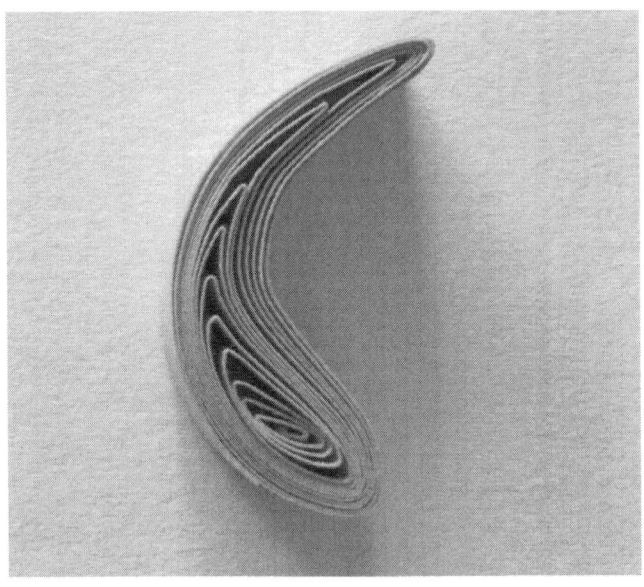

For a more obvious curved shape throughout, press the shape around your quilling tool. From here, you can easily create a paisley shape.

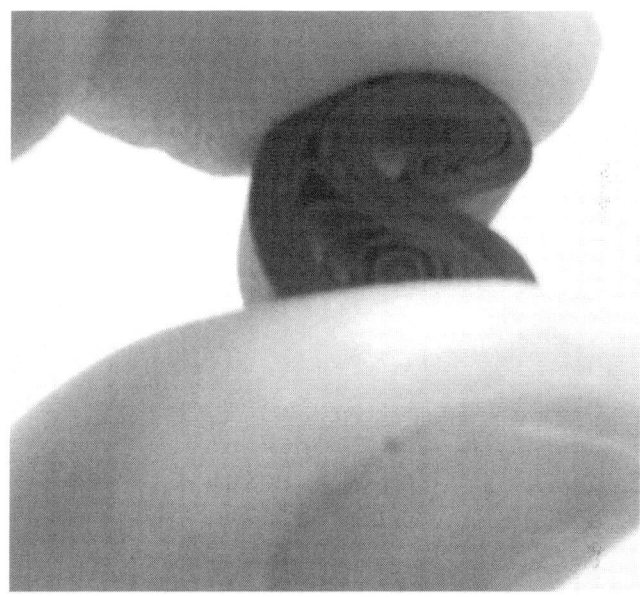

You can curl the shape from the point to the base by rolling it between your fingers.

So many shapes!

Marquis

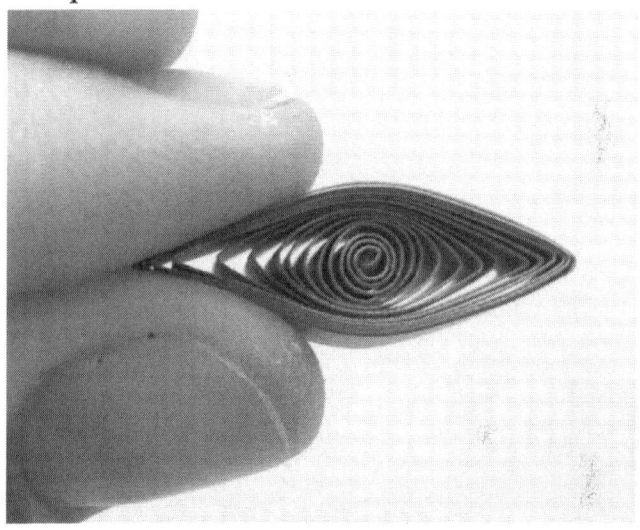

First make a teardrop shape, then pinch the opposite end as well.

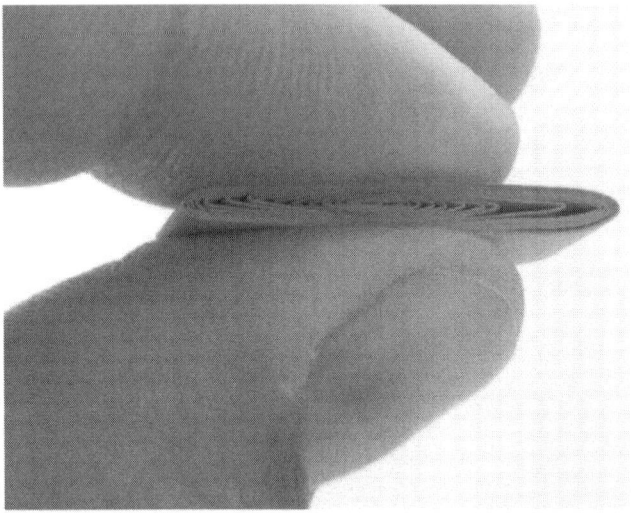

The final shape will be determined by how much you pinch or press the the coil together and where you place its center.

Paper Quilling Patterns Step by Step

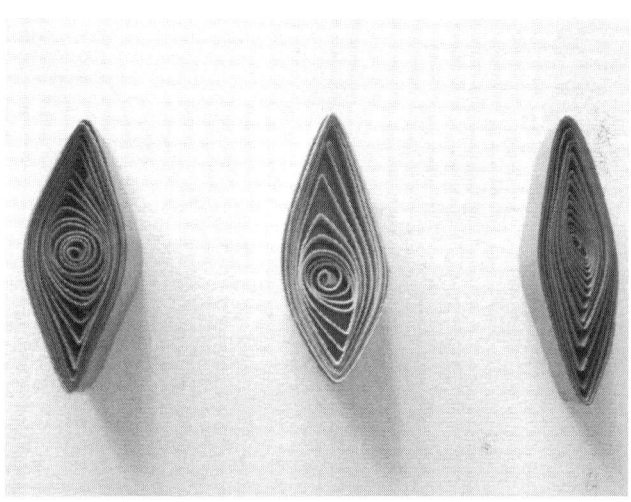

Play around with different placements and pressure to create lots of marquis versions.

Tulip

First make a marquis shape, then turn the shape on its side and pinch a center peak with your fingers.

Slug

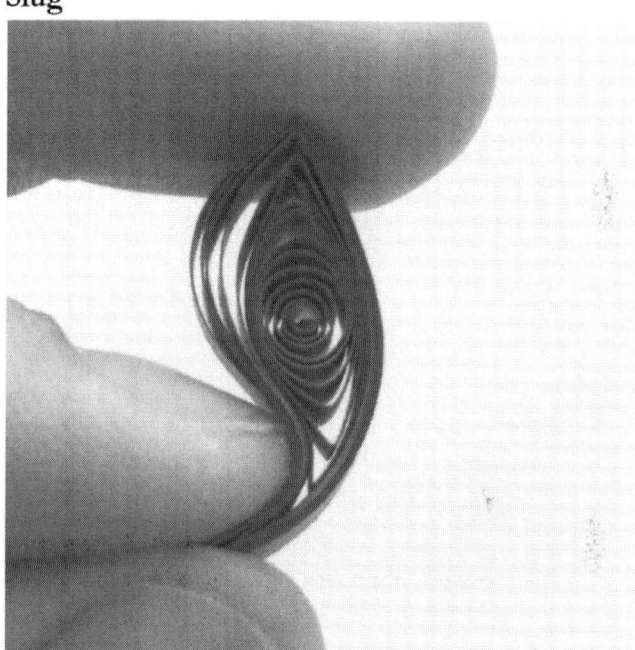

Start with a marquis, then wrap one end around the tip of your finger or a quilling tool.

Paper Quilling Patterns Step by Step

Do the same to the other end but in the opposite direction. Looks pretty for a slug, doesn't it!

Square or Diamond

Create a marquis shape, then rotate it 90 degrees and pinch both sides again. This will create a diamond shape.

If you want to continue on to making a square, gently open up the shape between your fingers.

Square Variations

By playing around with how much of each corner you choose to pinch when creating your square, you can get very different results.

Above left: By applying pressure to the outside corners, you can create a square with a rounded center.

Above center: This was made by completely pressing the open coil together on one side, then opening it up and pinching just the corners on the opposite side.

Above right: This got its unique center by completely pressing down the coil on both turns.

Yet another variation on the square: You can make these by applying pressure to the outside structure with your fingers or the stem of your quilling tool.

Rectangle

If you can make a square, you can make a rectangle. The difference is in how much you rotate the marquis shape before pinching additional angles.

Rotate it only slightly (rather than 90 degrees) before pinching and then open the shape to reveal the perfect rectangle.

Rectangle Variations

Alternately, you can create a quadrilateral shape by making your four corners at uneven intervals.

This shape is especially useful when you're making quilled paper mosaics and you need to fill in an odd space.

Semi-Circle

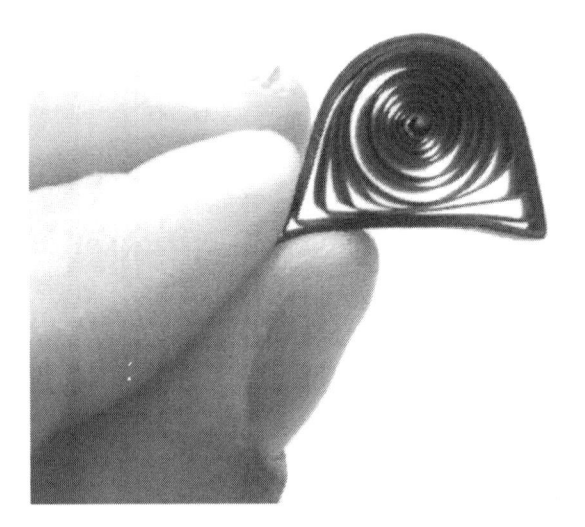

Start with an open coil, then pinch two corners while leaving the paper above them round. You can also do this by pressing an open coil onto a hard surface like a table and sliding your fingers down the sides carefully. Try both methods to see which suits you best.

Paper Quilling Patterns Step by Step

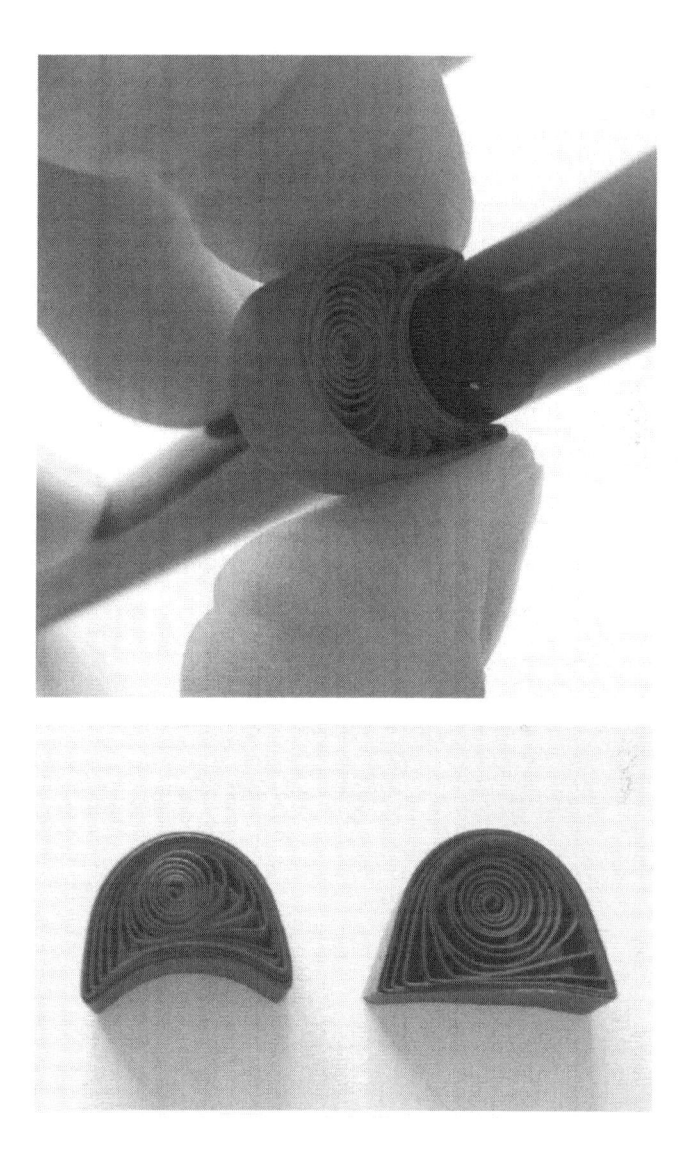

Curving the straight edge of the shape will allow you to turn a semi-circle into more of a crescent moon shape.

Triangle

Make a teardrop shape, then pinch two additional angles using either your fingers or the tabletop method.

Once again, try both to see what works best for you.

Triangle Variation

To create a shape that resembles a shark fin, press in two sides of your triangle and leave the third side flat.

Arrow

Make a teardrop, then pull the center down towards the base and hold it in place with your fingers.

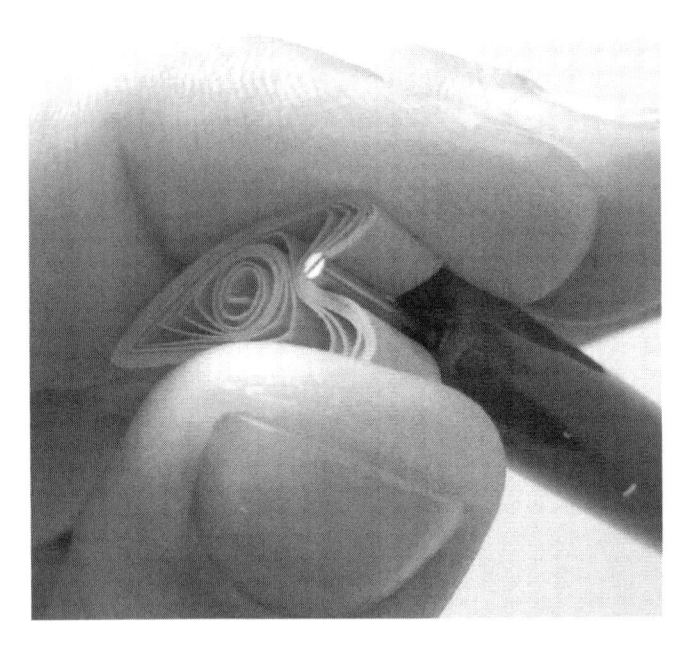

Using the long side of the slotted needle, press down deeply into the base.

Release the tool and smooth the curve out with your fingers to shape.

Arrowhead

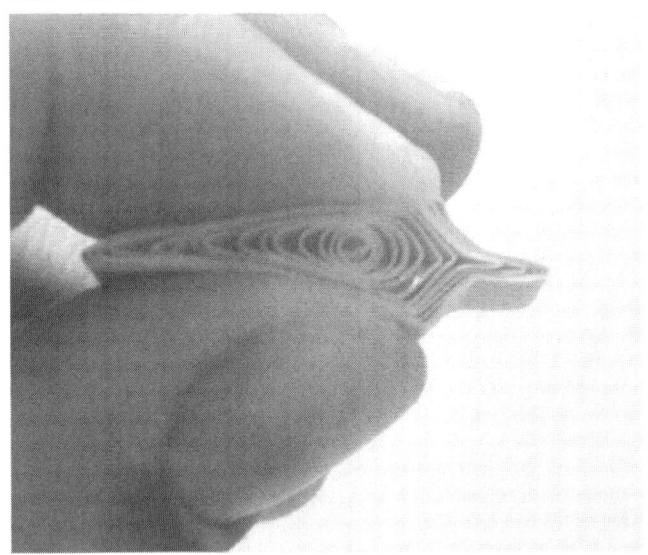

Beginning with a teardrop shape, hold the pointed end in your non-dominant hand and pinch the base end into a tight point.

Without letting go, slide your fingers down to meet the fingers of your opposite hand to create the side angles.

Heart

Once again, begin with a teardrop. Press in the base of the shape by using the point of your quilling tool to make a small indentation.

Release the tool and carefully press in each side of the heart to complete the center crease.

Pentagon and Star

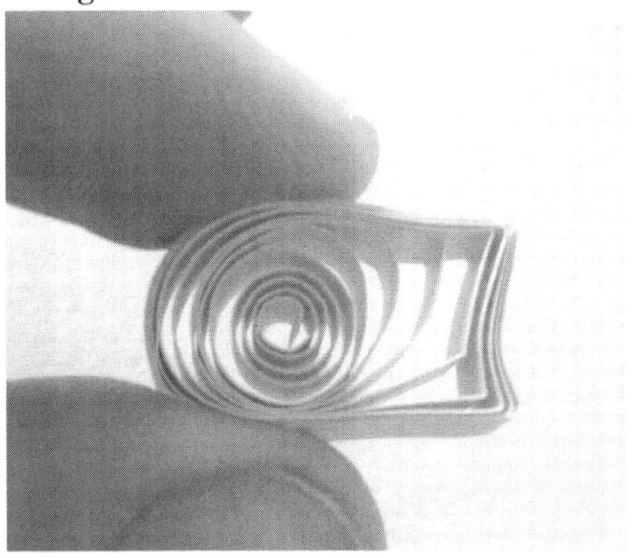

To make a pentagon, first create an elongated semi-circle as shown above.

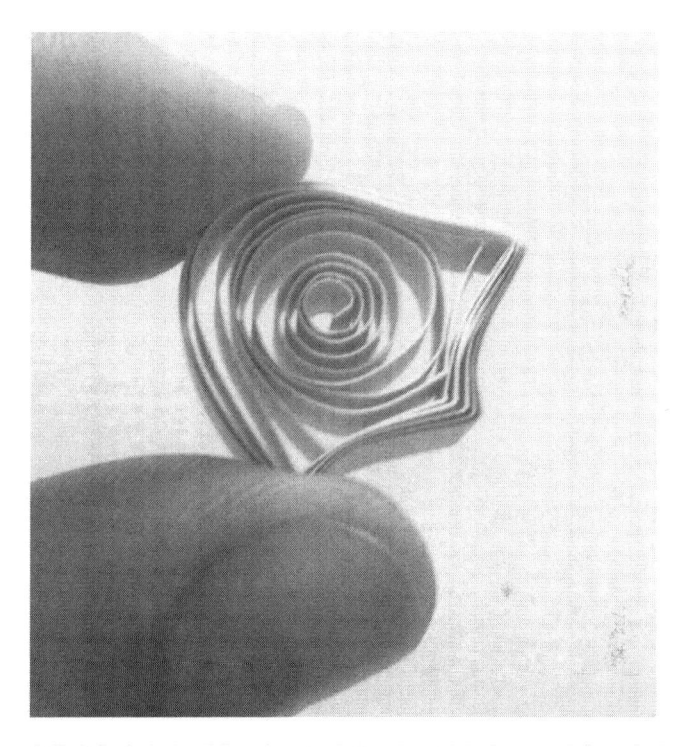

Pinch the center of the flat side using the same method you used when making the tulip shape; this is the peak of your pentagon.

Keeping the peak in the center, square off the bottom with two equal pinches on either side.

To turn the pentagon into a star, press in on each flat surface with your fingers or a quilling tool and then further refine each angle into peaks.

Holly Leaf

This shape is far and away the most difficult to create. For sanity's sake, you'll want to become comfortable making all of the other shapes before attempting this one!

Begin by making a marquis. Insert a set of tweezers into the shape; try to grip only about a third of the inside coil.

Keeping the grip with your tweezers, turn the marquis as needed and pinch a small point on either side of each peak.

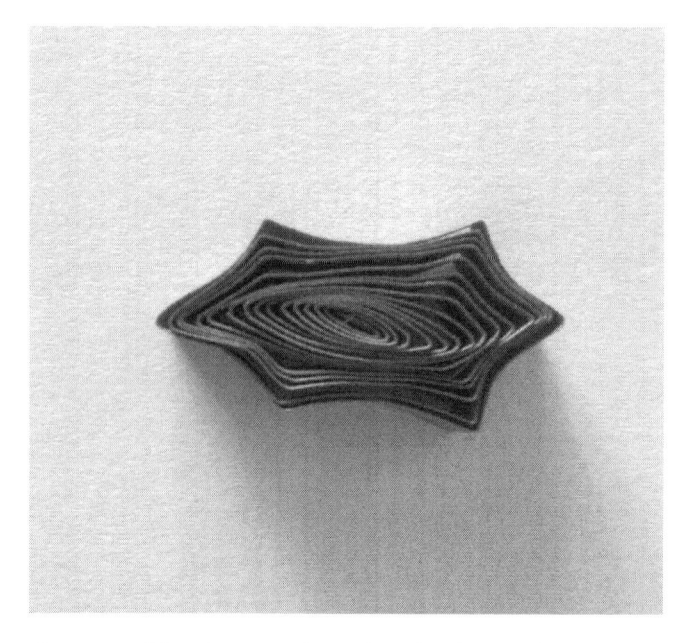

You could also make the holly leaf by first making a square, adding a point to each end and then shaping all the angles into peaks. I find the tweezer method easier, but try both ways to see which gives you better results.

Paper Quilling Patterns Step by Step

Printed in Great Britain
by Amazon